Light relief between grades

Spaß und Entspannung mit leichten Originalstücken für Violoncello *Erster Schwierigkeitsgrad*
Plaisir et détente avec des pièces originales simples pour piano *Niveau 1*

Cello part

Pam Wedgwood

FABER *ff* MUSIC

Foreword

Up-Grade! is a collection of new pieces and duets in a wide variety of styles for cellists of any age. This book is designed to be especially useful to students who have passed Grade 1 and would like a break before plunging into the syllabus for Grade 2.

Whether you're looking for stimulating material to help bridge the gap between grades, or simply need a bit of light relief, I hope you'll enjoy **Up-Grade!**

Pam Wedgwood

© 2000 by Faber Music Ltd
First published in 2000 by Faber Music Ltd
Bloomsbury House 74–77 Great Russell Street London WC1B 3DA
Cover design by Stik
Music processed by Jackie Leigh
Printed in England by Caligraving Ltd

ISBN10: 0-571-51962-8
EAN13: 978-0-571-51962-0

To buy Faber Music publications or to find out about the full range of titles available please contact your local music retailer or Faber Music sales enquiries:

Faber Music Limited, Burnt Mill, Elizabeth Way, Harlow CM20 2HX
Tel: +44 (0)1279 82 89 82   Fax: +44 (0)1279 82 89 83
sales@fabermusic.com   fabermusicstore.com

Contents

1. Take It Easy

Pamela Wedgwood

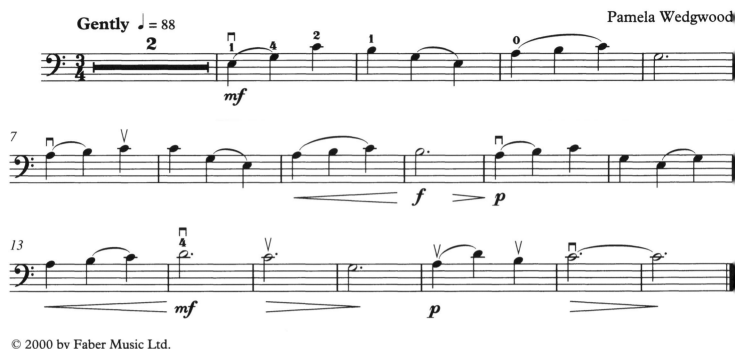

Gently ♩ = 88

2. Off to the Sun

Pamela Wedgwood

With a gentle breeze – relaxed ♩ = 120

3. Apple Pie Waltz

Relaxed and sugary ♩ = 104

Pamela Wedgwood

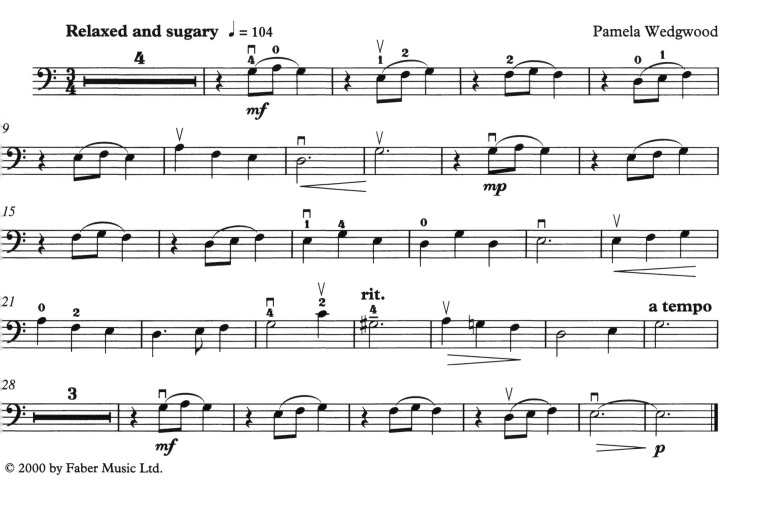

© 2000 by Faber Music Ltd.

4. Land of Hope and Glory

Maestoso (majestically) ♩ = 88

Edward Elgar

5. What shall we do with the Drunken Sailor?

Traditional

6. Tinkerbell

Pamela Wedgwood

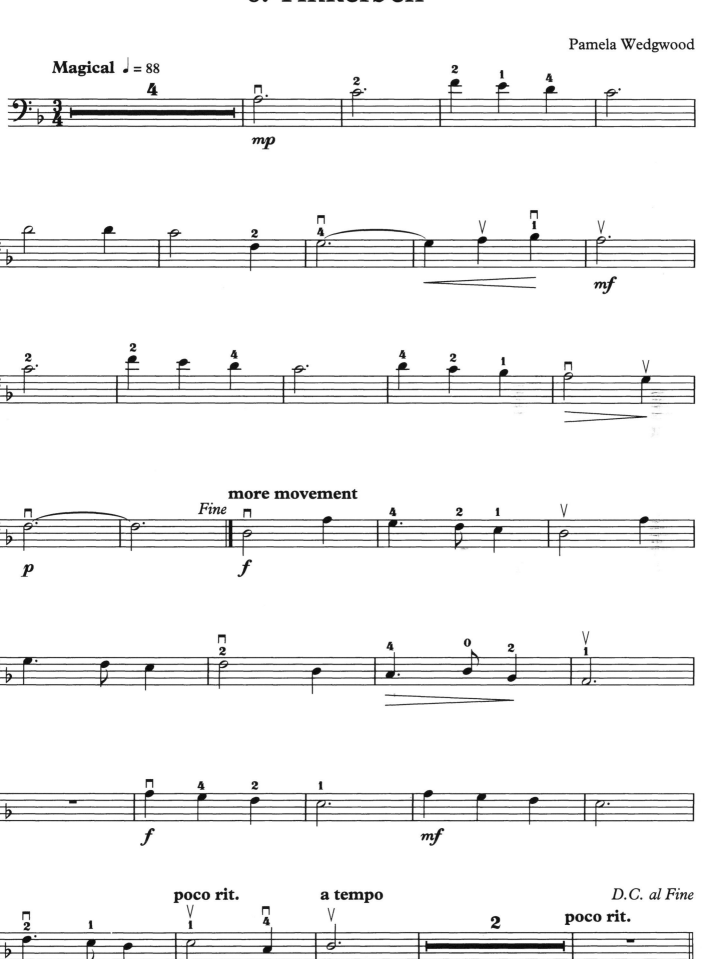

for Jack

7. Free Style

Pamela Wedgwood

Light relief between grades

Spaß und Entspannung mit leichten Originalstücken für Violoncello *Erster Schwierigkeitsgrad*
Plaisir et détente avec des pièces originales simples pour piano *Niveau 1*

Piano accompaniments

Pam Wedgwood

FABER *ff* MUSIC

Foreword

Up-Grade! is a collection of new pieces and duets in a wide variety of styles for cellists of any age. This book is designed to be especially useful to students who have passed Grade 1 and would like a break before plunging into the syllabus for Grade 2.

Whether you're looking for stimulating material to help bridge the gap between grades, or simply need a bit of light relief, I hope you'll enjoy **Up-Grade!**

Pam Wedgwood

© 2000 by Faber Music Ltd
First published in 2000 by Faber Music Ltd
Bloomsbury House 74–77 Great Russell Street London WC1B 3DA
Cover design by Stik
Music processed by Jackie Leigh
Printed in England by Caligraving Ltd
All rights reserved

ISBN10: 0-571-51962-8
EAN13: 978-0-571-51962-0

To buy Faber Music publications or to find out about the full range of titles available
please contact your local music retailer or Faber Music sales enquiries:

Faber Music Limited, Burnt Mill, Elizabeth Way, Harlow CM20 2HX
Tel: +44 (0)1279 82 89 82   Fax: +44 (0)1279 82 89 83
sales@fabermusic.com   fabermusicstore.com

Contents   page

1. Take It Easy

Pamela Wedgwood

2. Off to the Sun

With a gentle breeze – relaxed ♩ = 120

Pamela Wedgwood

3. Apple Pie Waltz

Pamela Wedgwood

4. Land of Hope and Glory

Edward Elgar

5. What shall we do with the Drunken Sailor?

Traditional

6. Tinkerbell

Pamela Wedgwood

for Jack

7. Free Style

Pamela Wedgwood

CODA

8. Daydream

Pamela Wedgwood

9. Rosemary and Thyme

Pamela Wedgwood

10. The Contented Frog

Pamela Wedgwood

11. Coconut Calypso

With a moderately gentle breeze ♩ = 108

Pamela Wedgwood

12. Siberian Galop

Pamela Wedgwood

8. Daydream

Pamela Wedgwood

9. Rosemary and Thyme

Pamela Wedgwood

10. The Contented Frog

Pamela Wedgwood

11. Coconut Calypso

With a moderately gentle breeze ♩ = 108

Pamela Wedgwood

12. Siberian Galop

13. Seaside Days

1. Splashing About

Pamela Wedgwood

2. Punch and Judy

3. Bucket and Spade Blues